KNIT
BABY AFGHANS
BY THE POUND

by Rita Weiss

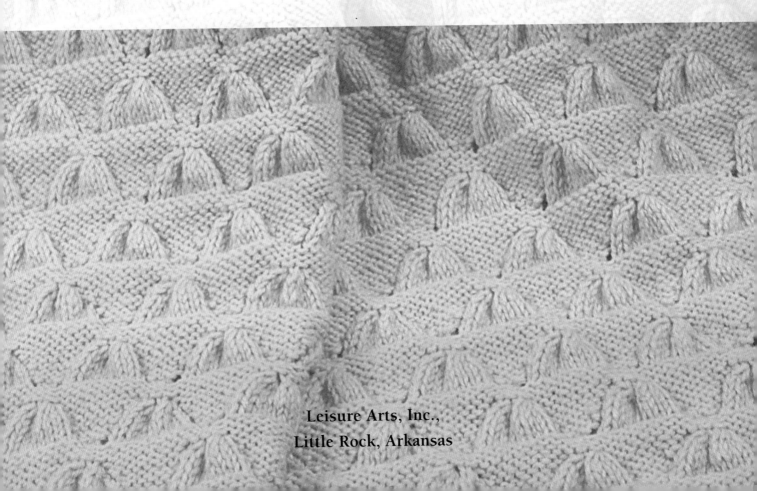

Leisure Arts, Inc.,
Little Rock, Arkansas

Produced by

Production Team

Creative Directors: Jean Leinhauser
and Rita Weiss

Senior Technical Editor: Ellen W. Liberles

Photographer: Carol Wilson Mansfield

Pattern Testers: Kim Britt, Carrie Cristiano,
Mary Ann Frits, Patricia Honaker,
Debra Hughes, Wendy Meier and
Kathy Wesley

Book Design: Linda Causee

Published by Leisure Arts

© 2011 by Leisure Arts, Inc.,

5701 Ranch Drive

Little Rock, AR 72223

www.leisurearts.com

Introduction

"How many pounds did the baby weigh?" is almost the first question we ask when we hear about a new baby. This is because a baby's weight may have some indication as to the baby's health.

Just as a baby's birth weight may be important, so is the weight of these afghans. For they are made with either one pound or two pounds of yarn. In this book, we have used the wonderfully convenient yarn skeins that weigh exactly one pound each – nice fat skeins that mean you never run out of yarn when you take your knitting with you wherever you go.

Nothing gets a knitter's fingers itching to be stitching more than learning a new baby is soon to arrive. Visions of blankets or afghans start dancing around, and soon the search for the perfect pattern begins.

This collection is bright and fun, with interesting stitch patterns and colors that are sure to spice up any nursery. Most of the afghans in this collection are easy enough for the beginning knitter, but they are sure to win the accolades of the new mother. If you are a more experienced knitter, there are a few afghans here that will keep the advanced knitter happy as well.

One of these designs may become baby's best friend, a familiar comfort that is dragged around and cuddled up with at nap time. And your hand-crafted welcome gift will be the hit of any baby shower.

So get out your knitting needles, a pound (or two) of yarn, and start making something for that cherished baby to enjoy. No matter the size of the baby, the parents will appreciate your gift of a warm, blanket for their pride and joy.

MERRY-GO-ROUND

Skill Level: Intermediate ◼◼◼◻

Size

Appoximately 34" (86 cm) in diameter

Materials

Worsted Weight Yarn

[100% acrylic, 16 ounces, 1020 yards
(449 grams, 932 meters) per skein]

   1 skein yellow

Note: *Photographed model made with Lion Brand®
Pound of Love® #157 Pastel Yellow*

Four size 8 (5 mm) double point needles (or
size required for gauge)

36" size 8 (5 mm) circular knitting needle (or
size required for gauge)

Note: *Begin afghan with double-point needles and
switch to circular needle when the number of sts
increases*

Gauge

18 sts = 4" (10 cm) in stockinette stitch (knit 1
row, purl 1 row)

INSTRUCTIONS

CO 12 sts onto one double-point needle. Divide
the sts onto three double-point needles. Join,
being careful not to twist stitches, and knit two
rnds even. Change to circular needles when
necessary.

Rnd 1: *(YO) twice, K1; rep from * around:
36 sts.

Rnd 2: Knit around, knitting first YO and
allowing second YO to drop: 24 sts.

Rnd 3: *(YO) twice, K2; rep from * around:
48 sts.

Rnd 4: Rep Rnd 2: 36 sts.

Rnd 5: *(YO) twice, K3; rep from * around:
60 sts.

Rnd 6: Rep Rnd 2: 48 sts.

Rnd 7: *(YO) twice, K4; rep from * around:
72 sts.

Rnd 8: Rep Rnd 2: 60 sts.

Rnd 9: *(YO) twice, K5; rep from * around:
84 sts.

Rnd 10: Rep Rnd 2: 72 sts.

Rnd 11: *(YO) twice, K6; rep from * around:
96 sts.

Rnd 12: Rep Rnd 2: 84 sts

Rnd 13: *(YO) twice, K7; rep from * around:
108 sts.

Rnd 14: Rep Rnd 2: 96 sts.

Rnd 15: *(YO) twice, K8; rep from * around:
120 sts.

Rnd 16: Rep Rnd 2: 108 sts

Rnd 17: *(YO) twice, K1, (YO) twice, sl 1, K1,
PSSO, K6; rep from * around: 144 sts.

Rnd 18: Rep Rnd 2: 120 sts.

Rnd 19: *(YO) twice, K3, (YO) twice, sl 1, K1,
PSSO, K5; rep from * around: 156 sts.

Rnd 20: Rep Rnd 2: 132 sts.

Rnd 21: *(YO) twice, K5, (YO) twice, sl 1, K1,
PSSO, K4; rep from * around: 168 sts.

Rnd 22: Rep Rnd 2: 144 sts.

Rnd 23: *(YO) twice, K7, (YO) twice, sl 1, K1,
PSSO, K3; rep from * around: 180 sts.

Instructions continued on page 6.

Rnd 24: Rep Rnd 2: 156 sts.

Rnd 25: *(YO) twice, K1, (YO) twice, sl 1, K1, PSSO **, K3, K2tog; rep from * to ** once, K2***; rep from * to *** around: 216 sts.

Rnd 26: Rep Rnd 2: 168 sts.

Rnd 27: *(YO) twice, K3, (YO) twice, sl 1, K1, PSSO, K1**, K2tog***; rep from * to ** once; rep from * to *** around: 228 sts.

Rnd 28: Rep Rnd 2: 180 sts.

Rnd 29: *(YO) twice, K5, (YO) twice, ** sl 1, K2tog, PSSO. Rep from * to ** once, K2tog, rep from * around: 240 sts.

Rnd 30: Rep Rnd 2: 192 sts.

Rnd 31: *(YO) twice, K3, K2tog, K2, (YO) twice, K1, (YO) twice, K2, K2tog, K3, (YO) twice, K1; rep from * around: 264 sts.

Rnd 32: Rep Rnd 2: 216 sts.

Rnds 33 and 34: Knit around.

Rnd 35: *YO, K1, YO, K2, (K2 tog) twice, (K1, YO) 3 times, K2, (K2tog) twice, K1, YO, K1; rep from * around : 240 sts.

Rnds 36 through 38: Knit around.

Rnd 39: *(K1, YO) twice, K1, (K2tog) 3 times, YO, K1, YO; rep from * around: 264 sts.

Rnds 40 through 42: Knit around.

Rnd 43: *(K1, YO) twice, K1, (K2tog) 3 times, (K1, YO) twice; rep from * around: 288 sts.

Rnds 44 through 46: Knit around.

Rnd 47: *(K1, YO) 3 times, (K2tog) 4 times, YO, K1, YO; rep from * around: 312 sts.

Rnds 48 through 50: Knit around.

Rnd 51: *(K1, YO) 3 times, K1, (K2tog) 4 times, YO, K1, YO; rep from * around: 336 sts.

Rnds 52 through 54: Knit around.

Rnd 55: *(K1, YO) 3 times, K1, (K2tog) 4 times, (K1, YO) twice; rep from * around: 360 sts.

Rnds 56 through 58: Knit around.

Rnd 59: *(K1, YO) 3 times, (K2tog) 5 times, (YO, K1) twice, YO; rep fron * around: 384 sts.

Rnds 60 through 62: Knit around.

Rnd 63: *(K1, YO) 3 times, K1, (K2tog) 5 times, (YO, K1) twice, YO; rep from * around: 408 sts.

Rnds 64 through 66: Knit around.

Rnd 67: *(K1, YO) 3 times, K1, (K2tog) 5 times, (K1, YO) 3 times; rep from * around: 432 sts.

Rnds 68 though 70: Knit around.

Rnd 71: *(K1, YO) 4 times, (K2tog) 6 times, (YO, K1) twice, YO; rep from * around: 456 sts.

Rnds 72 through 74: Knit around.

Rnd 75: *(K1, YO) 4 times, K1, (K2tog) 6 times, (YO, K1) twice; rep from * around: 456 sts.

Rnd 76 through 79: Knit around.

Rnd 80: *(K1, YO) 4 times, K1, (K2tog) 6 times, (YO, K1) twice, YO; rep from * around: 480 sts.

Rnds 81 through 84: Knit around.

Rnd 85: *(K1, YO) 4 times, K1, (K2tog) 6 times, (K1, YO) 3 times; rep from * around: 504 sts

Rnds 86 through 89: Knit around.

Rnd 90: *(K1, YO) 4 times, (K2tog) 7 times, (YO, K1) 3 times, YO; rep from * around: 528 sts.

Rnds 91 through 94: Knit around.

Rnd 95: *(K1, YO) 4 times, K1, (K2tog) 7 times, (YO, K1) 3 times, YO; rep from * around: 552 sts.

Rnds 96 through 99: Knit around.

Rnd 100: *(YO, K1) 4 times, K1, (K2tog) 7 times, (YO, K1) 4 times; rep from * around: 576 sts.

Rnds 101 though 104: Knit around.

Rnd 105: *(K1, YO) 5 times, (K2tog) 8 times, (YO, K1) 3 times, YO; rep from * around: 600 sts.

Rnds 106 to 109: Knit around.

Rnd 110: Purl around.

BO all sts; weave in all yarn ends.

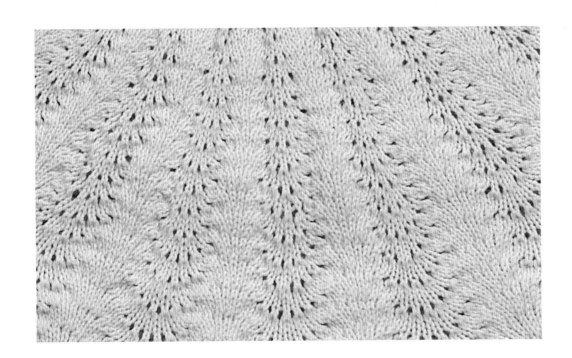

7

Blue Bells

Skill Level: Easy

Size

Approximately 36" x 40" (91 cm x 102 cm)

Materials

Worsted Weight Yarn

[100% acrylic, 16 ounces, 1020 yards (449 grams, 932 meters) per skein]

   1 skein blue

Note: *Photographed model made with Lion Brand® Pound of Love® #106 Pastel Blue*

36" size 8 (5 mm) circular knitting needle (or size required for gauge)

Gauge

18 sts = 4" (10 cm) in stockinette st (knit 1 row, purl 1 row)

INSTRUCTIONS

CO 146 sts. Do not join; work back and forth in rows.

Rows 1 through 4: Knit.

Row 5 (right side): K3; *P1, YO, K8, YO, P1; rep from * to last 3 sts, K3.

Row 6: K3; *K2, P8, K2; rep from * to last 3 sts, K3.

Row 7: K3; *P2, YO, K8, YO, P2; rep from * to last 3 sts, K3.

Row 8: K3; *K3, P8, K3; rep from * to last 3 sts, K3.

Row 9: K3; *P3, YO, K8, YO, P3; rep from * to last 3 sts, K3.

Row 10: K3; *K4, P8, K4; rep from * to to last 3 sts, K3.

Row 11: K3; *P4, (K4tog) twice, P4; rep from * to last 3 sts, K3.

Row 12: Knit.

Row 13: K3, purl to last 3 sts, K3.

Row 14: Knit.

Row 15: K3, K4, YO, P1; *P1, YO, K8, YO, P1; rep from * to last 8 sts, P1, YO, K7.

Row 16: K3, P4, K2; *K2, P8, K2; rep from * to last 9 sts, K2, P4, K3.

Row 17: K3, K4, YO, P2; *P2, YO, K8, YO, P2; rep from * to last 9 sts, P2, YO, K7.

Instructions continued on page 10.

Row 18: K3, P4, K3; *K3, P8, K3; rep from * to last 10 sts K3, P4, K3.

Row 19: K7, YO, P3; *P3, YO, K8, YO, P3; rep from * to last 10 sts, P3, YO, K7.

Row 20: K3. P4, K4; *K4, P8, K4; rep from * to last 11sts, K4, P4, K3.

Row 21: K3, K4tog, P4; *P4, (K4tog) twice, P4; rep from * to last 11 sts, P4, K4tog, K3

Row 22: Knit.

Row 23: K3, purl to last 3 sts, K3.

Row 24: Knit.

Repeat Rows 5 through 24 until afghan measures approximately 40" (102 cm), ending by working Row 14.

BO; weave in all yarn ends.

BABY CABLES
Skill Level: Intermediate

Size
Approx 36" x 38" (91 cm x 97 cm)

Materials
Worsted Weight Yarn

[100% acrylic, 16 ounces, 1020 yards
(449 grams, 932 meters) per skein]

    1 skein pink

Note: *Photographed model made with Lion Brand®
Pound of Love® #101 Pastel Pink*

36" size 8 (5 mm) circular knitting needle (or
size required for gauge)

Cable Needle

Gauge
18 sts = 4" (10 cm) in stockinette st (knit 1
row, purl 1 row)

Stitch Guide
C4F (Cable 4 Front): Slip next 2 sts to cable
needle and hold at front, K2, then K2 from
cable needle.

C4B (Cable 4 Back): Slip next 2 sts to cable
needle and hold at back, K2, then K2 from cable
needle.

INSTRUCTIONS
CO 172 sts. Do not join; work back and forth in
rows.

Knit 6 rows.

Row 1 (right side): K5; *P2, K8, P2, K8; rep
from * to last 7 sts, P2, K5.

Row 2: K6; *P8, K2; rep from * to last 6 sts, K6.

Row 3: K5; *P2, K8, P2, K1, (sl 1, K1, PSSO,
YO) 3 times, K1; rep from * to last 7 sts, P2, K5.

Row 4: K6; *P8, K2; rep from * to last 6 sts, K6.

Row 5: K5; *P2, K8, P2, (sl 1, K1, PSSO, YO) 3
times, K2; rep from * to last 7 sts, P2, K5.

Instructions continued on page 13

Row 6: K6; *P8, K2; rep from * to last 6 sts, K6.

Row 7: K5; *P2, K8, P2, K1, (sl 1, K1, PSSO, YO) twice, K3: rep from * to last 7 sts, P2, K5.

Row 8: K6; *P8, K2; rep from * to last 6 sts, K6.

Row 9: K5, P2; *C4B, C4F, P2; rep from * to last 5 sts, K5.

Row 10: K6; *P8, K2; rep from * to last 6 sts, K6.

Row 11: K5; *P2, K1, (sl 1, K1, PSSO, YO) 3 times, K1, P2, K8; rep from * to last 7 sts, P2, K5.

Row 12: K6; *P8, K2; rep from * to last 6 sts, K6.

Row 13: K5; *P2, (sl 1, K1, PSSO, YO) 3 times, K2, P2, K8; rep from * to last 7 sts, P2, K5.

Row 14: K6; *P8, K2; rep from * to last 6 sts, K6.

Row 15: K5; *P2, K1, (sl 1, K1, PSSO, YO) twice, K3, P2, K8; rep from * to last 7 sts, P2, K5.

Row 16: K6; *P8, K2; rep from * to last 6 sts, K6.

Row 17: K5, P2; *C4B, C4F, P2; rep from * to last 5 sts, K5.

Row 18: K6; *P8, K2; rep from * to last 6 sts, K6.

Repeat Rows 3 through 18 until afghan measures about 39".

Next Row: K5, purl to last 5 sts, K5. Knit 5 rows.

BO; weave in all yarn ends.

SEA SHELLS
Skill Level: Intermediate

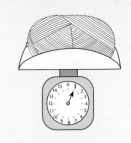

Size
36" x 40" (91 cm x 102 cm)

Materials
Worsted Weight Yarn
[100% acrylic, 16 ounces, 1020 yards (449 grams, 932 meters) per skein]

    1 skein white

Note: *Photographed model made with Lion Brand® Pound of Love® #099 Antique White*

36" Size 8 (5 mm) circular knitting needle (or size required for gauge)

Gauge
14 sts = 4" (10 cm) in garter st (knit each row)

INSTRUCTIONS
CO 177 sts. Do not join; work back and forth in rows.

Row 1: Knit.

Row 2: Knit.

Row 3: Knit.

Row 4 (right side): Knit.

Row 5: K3; *K1, YO, K2tog, K13, K2tog, YO, K1; rep from * to last 3 sts, K3.

Row 6: K3; *K1, (K1, P1 into YO), K15, (P1, K1 into YO), K1; rep from * to last 3 sts, K3.

Rows 7 and 8: Knit.

Row 9: K3; *K1; (YO, K2tog) twice, K11, (K2tog, YO) twice, K1; rep from * to last 3 sts, K3.

Row 10: K3; *[K1, (K1, P1 into YO)] twice, K13, [(P1, K1 into YO), K1] twice; rep from * to last 3 sts, K3.

Row 11: Knit.

Row 12: K3; *K6, [(YO) twice, K1] 14 times, K5; rep from * to last 3 sts, K3.

Row 13: K3; *K1, (YO, K2tog) twice, YO, slip next 15 sts to right-hand needle, allowing extra lps to drop. Slip these 15 sts back onto left-hand needle and purl all 15 sts tog; (YO, K2tog) twice, YO, K1; rep from * to last 3 sts, K3.

Row 14: K3; *[K1, (P1, K1 into YO)] three times, K1, [(K1, P1 into YO) K1] three times; rep from * to last 3 sts, K3.

Row 15: Knit.

Repeat Rows 4 through 15 for pattern until afghan measures approximately 39" (99 cm). Then knit 4 rows.

BO loosely; weave in all yarn ends.

NIGHTY NIGHT

Skill Level: Easy

Size

Approximately 37" x 37" (94 cm x 94 cm)

Materials

Worsted weight yarn ⑷

[100% acrylic, 16 ounces, 835 yards
(438 grams, 764 meters) per skein]

    1 skein peach

Note: *Photograped model made with Caron® One Pound #504 Peach*

36" size 8 circular knitting needle (or size required for gauge)

Gauge

18 sts = 4" (10 cm) in stockinette st (knit 1 row, purl 1 row)

INSTRUCTIONS

CO 139 sts. Do not join; work back and forth in rows.

Knit 4 rows.

Row 1(right side): K3, K2tog; *YO, K3, YO, sl 1, K2tog, PSSO; rep from * to last 8 sts, YO, K3, YO, sl 1, K1, PSSO, K3.

Row 2: K5; *P3, K3; rep from * to last 8 sts, P3, K5.

Row 3: K3, P2, *K3, P3; rep from * to last 8 sts, K3, P2, K3.

Row 4: Rep Row 2.

Row 5: K5; *YO, sl 1, K2tog, PSSO, YO, K3; rep from * to last 8 sts, YO, sl 1, K2tog, PSSO, YO, K5.

Row 6: K3, P2; *K3, P3; rep from * to last 8 sts, K3, P2, K3.

Row 7: K5; *P3, K3; rep from * to last 8 sts, P3, K5.

Row 8: Rep Row 6.

Repeat Rows 1 through 8 until piece measures approximately 36$\frac{1}{2}$" (93 cm), ending by working Row 5.

Knit 4 rows.

BO; weave in all yarn ends.

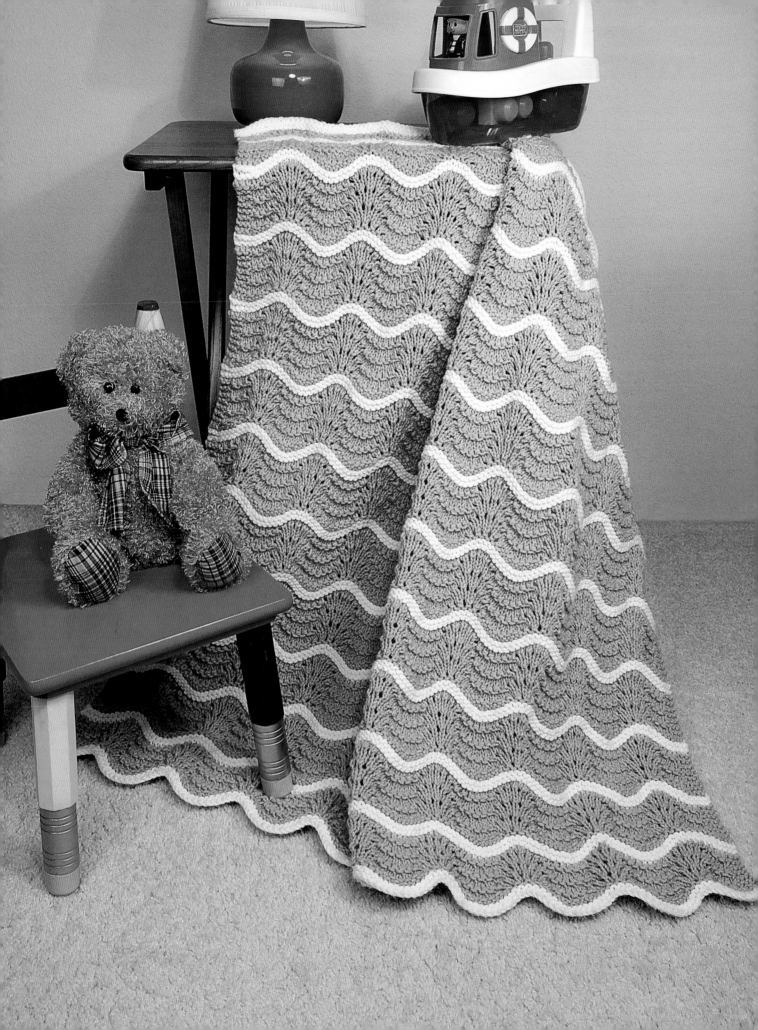

HIGH TIDE

Skill Level: Easy

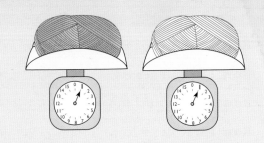

Size

Approximately 36" x 40" (91 cm x 102 cm)

Materials

Worsted weight yarn

[100% acrylic, 16 ounces, 835 yards
(438 grams, 764 meters) per skein]

　　1 skein white (A)

[100% acrylic, 16 ounces, 812 yards (453.6
grams, 742 meters) per skein]

　　1 skein blue (B)

Note: *Photographed model made with Red Heart®
Super Saver® #501 White(A) and Caron® One
Pound #381 Lt Blue(B)*

36" Size 8 (5mm) circular knitting needle (or
size required for gauge)

Gauge

18 sts = 4" (10 cm) in stockinette st (knit 1
row, purl 1 row)

INSTRUCTIONS

With Color A, CO 176 sts. Do not join; work
back and forth in rows.

Row 1: Knit across.

Row 2: Knit across. At end of row, cut Color A,
attach Color B.

Row 3: With Color B, knit across.

Row 4: Knit across.

Row 5 (right side): K3; *(P2tog) 3 times, (YO,
K1) 5 times, YO, (P2tog) 3 times; rep from * to
last 3 sts, K3.

Row 6: K3; purl to last 3 sts, K3.

Row 7: Knit across.

Row 8: K3; purl to last 3 sts, K3.

Row 9: K3; *(P2tog) 3 times, (YO, K1) 5 times,
YO, (P2tog) 3 times; rep from * to last 3 sts, K3.

Instructions continued on page 20.

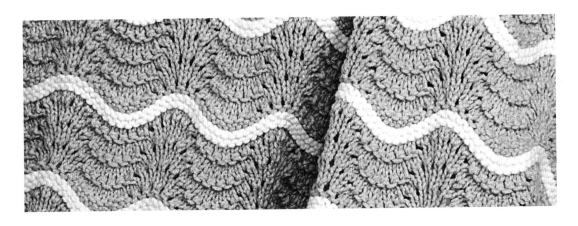

Row 10: K3; purl to last 3 sts, K3.

Row 11: Knit across.

Row 12: K3; purl to last 3 sts, K3.

Row 13: K3; *(P2tog) 3 times, (YO, K1) 5 times, YO, (P2tog) 3 times; rep from * to last 3 sts, K3.

Row 14: K3; purl to last 3 sts, K3.

Row 15: Knit across.

Row 16: K3; purl to last 3 sts, K3.

Row 17: K3; *(P2tog) 3 times, (YO, K1) 5 times, YO, (P2tog) 3 times; rep from * to last 3 sts, K3.

Row 18: K3; purl to last 3 sts, K3. At end of row, cut Color B; attach Color A.

Rows 19 through 22: With Color A, Knit. At end of Row 22, cut Color A; attach Color B.

Repeat Rows 3 through 22 until afghan is about 40" (102 cm) ending by working Row 22.

BO; weave in all yarn ends.

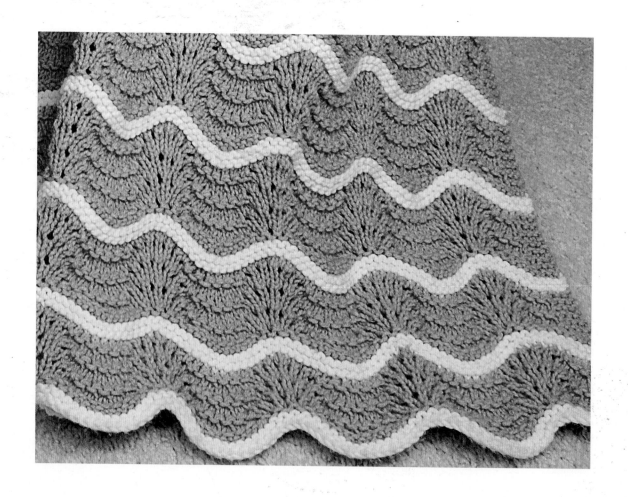

SUNFLOWER GARDEN
Skill Level: Intermediate

 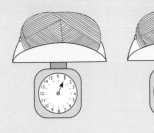 

Size
45" x 45" (11

[handwritten note: 149 CAST ON — 15 ST EACH REPEAT — 9 REPEATS — tally marks]

Materials
Worsted weig
[100% acryli
(453.6 grams

2 skeins ye

Note: *Photogr*   *n® One*
Pound #549 Su

36" size 8 (5
size required f

Gauge
14 st = 4" (10 cm) in garter st (knit every row)

Stitch Guide

BB (Bobble): (K1, P1) twice in same st; turn, P4; pass 2nd, 3rd and 4th sts one at a time over first st; turn, then knit into back of this st: BB made.

INSTRUCTIONS

CO 179 sts. Do not join; work back and forth in rows.

Knit 10 rows for border.

Row 1: K7; *P5, K2, P1, K2, P5; rep from to last 7 sts, K7.

Row 2: K7; *K5, P2, K1, P2, K5; rep from * to last 7 sts, K7.

Row 3: K7; *P4, K2tog, K1, YO, P1, YO, K1, sl 1, K1, PSSO, P4; rep from * to last 7sts, K7.

Row 4: K7; *K4, P3, K1, P3, K4; rep from * to last 7 sts, K7.

Row 5: K7; *P3, K2tog, K1, YO, K1, P1, K1, YO, K1, sl 1, K1, PSSO, P3; rep from * to last 7 sts, K7.

Row 6: K7; *K3, P4, K1, P4, K3; rep from * to last 7 sts, K7.

Row 7: K7; *P2, K2tog, K1, YO, K2, P1, K2, YO, K1, sl 1, K1, PSSO, P2; rep from * to last 7 sts, K7.

Row 8: K7; *K2, P5, K1, P5, K2; rep from * to last 7 sts, K7.

Row 9: K7; *P1, K2tog, K1, YO, K3, P1, K3, YO, K1, sl 1, K1, PSSO, P1 rep from * to last 7 sts, K7.

Row 10: K7; * K1, P6, K1, P6, K1; rep from * to last 7 sts, K7.

Instructions continued on page 23.

Row 11: K7, *K2tog, K1, YO, K1, K2tog, (K1, YO) twice, K1, sl 1, K1, PSSO, K1, YO, K1, sl 1, K1, PSSO; rep from * to last 7 sts, K7.

Row 12: K7; *P6, K1, P1, K1, P6; rep from * to last 7 sts, K7.

Row 13: K7; *K3, K2tog, K1, YO, P1, K1, P1, YO, K1, sl 1, K1, PSSO, K3; rep from * to last 7 sts, K7.

Row 14: K7; *P5, K2, P1, K2, P5; rep from * to last 7 sts, K7.

Row 15: K7; *K2, K2tog, K1, YO, P2, K1, P2, YO, K1, sl 1, K1, PSSO, K2; rep from * to last 7 sts, K7.

Row 16: K7; *P4, K3, P1, K3, P4; rep from * to last 7 sts, K7.

Row 17: K7; *K1, K2tog, K1, YO, P3, K1, P3, YO, K1, sl 1, K1, PSSO, K1; rep from * to last 7 sts, K7.

Row 18: K7; *P3, K4, P1, K4, P3; rep from * to last 7 sts, K7.

Row 19: K7; *K2tog, K1, YO, P3, BB, P1, BB, P3, YO, K1, sl 1, K1, PSSO; rep from * to last 7 sts, K7.

Row 20: K7; *P1, K13, P1; rep from * to last 7 sts, K7.

Row 21: K7; *P4, BB, P5, BB, P4; rep from * to last 7 sts, K7.

Row 22: Knit across.

Row 23: K7; *P3, BB, P1, (P2tog, YO) twice, P2, BB, P3; rep from * to last 7 sts, K7.

Row 24: Knit across.

Row 25: K7; *P3, BB, (P2tog, YO) 3 times, P1, BB, P3; rep from * to last 7 sts, K7.

Row 26: Knit across.

Row 27: K7; *P3, BB, P1, (P2tog, YO) twice, P2, BB, P3; rep from * to last 7 sts, K7.

Row 28: Knit across.

Row 29: K7; *P4, BB, P5, BB, P4; rep from * to last 7 sts, K7.

Row 30: Knit.

Row 31: K7; *P6, BB, P1, BB, P6; rep from * to last 7 sts, K7.

Row 32: Knit.

Repeat Rows 1 through 32 six times more, until piece measures approximately 43" (109 cm).

Knit 10 rows.

BO; weave in all yarn ends.

23

SWEET VALENTINE
Skill Level: Intermediate

Size
Approximately 40" x 44" (102 cm x 112 cm)

Materials
Worsted weight yarn
[100% acrylic, 16 ounces, 812 yards (453.6 grams, 742 meters) per skein]

    1 skein scarlet

Note: *Photographed model made with Caron® One Pound #516 Scarlett*

36" Size 8 (5 mm) circular knitting needle (or size required for gauge)

Gauge
18 sts = 4" (10 cm) in stockinette (knit 1 row, purl 1 row)

INSTRUCTIONS
CO 124 sts. Do not join; work back and forth in rows.

Row 1: Knit.

Row 2 (wrong side): Purl.

Row 3: K2; *K3, YO, sl 1 as to knit, K2tog, PSSO, YO; rep from * to last 2 sts, K2.

Row 4: Purl.

Row 5: K2; *YO, sl 1 as to knit, K2tog, PSSO, YO, K3; rep from * to last 2 sts, K2.

Rep Rows 2 through 5 until piece measures approx 44" (112 cm) from CO edge, ending by working Row 2. BO until 1 st remains on needle.

EDGING
With right side facing and CO sts along bottom and BO sts at top, work in edge sts along sides. *YO, sk next st, knit next st: 3 sts; turn; sl 1 tightly, work (K1, P1, K1) in next st, P1: 5 sts; turn. BO 4 sts (leaving 1 st on needle). Rep from * around outer edge to last st, YO, sk last st, pick up and knit in first st of border; turn; sl 1 tightly, (K1, P1, K1) in next st, P1. turn.

BO all 5 sts. Weave in all yarn ends.

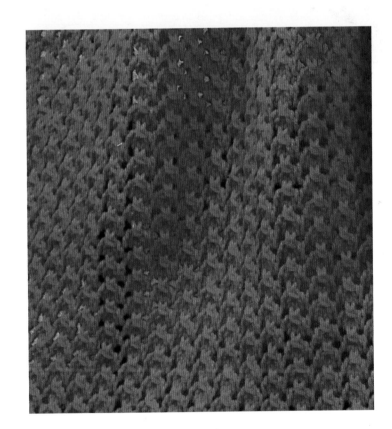

COMING UP ROSES
Skill Level: Easy

Size

Approximately 36" x 40" (91 cm x 102 cm)

Materials

Worsted weight yarn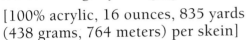

[100% acrylic, 16 ounces, 835 yards
(438 grams, 764 meters) per skein]

    1 skein rose

Note: *Photograped model made with Caron® One
Pound #517 Rose*

36" size 8 circular knitting needle (or size
required for gauge)

Gauge

18 sts = 4" (10 cm) in stockinette st (knit 1 row,
purl 1 row)

INSTRUCTIONS

CO 145 sts. Do not join; work back and forth
in rows.

Rows 1 through 8: *K1, P1; rep from * across
ending with K1.

Row 9: (K1, P1) three times, K1; *YO, K1, sl 1,
K1, PSSO, K5, K2tog, K1,YO, K1; rep from * to
last 6 sts, (P1, K1) three times.

Row 10: (K1, P1) three times, K1, purl to last 7
sts, (K1, P1) 3 times, K1.

Row 11: (K1, P1) three times, *K2, YO, K1, sl
1, K1, PSSO, K3, K2tog, K1, YO, K1; rep from *
to last 7 sts, (K1, P1) 3 times, K1.

Row 12: Rep Row 10.

Row 13: (K1, P1) 3 times, *K3, YO, K1, sl 1,
K1, PSSO, K1, K2tog, K1, YO, K2; rep from * to
last 7 sts, (K1, P1) 3 times, K1.

Row 14: Rep Row 10.

Row 15: (K1, P1) 3 times, *K4, YO, K1, sl 1,
K2tog, PSSO, K1, YO, K3; rep from * to last 7
sts, (K1, P1) 3 times, K1.

Row 16: Rep Row 10.

Rep Rows 9 through 16 until afghan measures
approx 39" (99 cm), ending by working Row
15. Then work Rows 1 through 7.

BO all sts; weave in all yarn ends.

SPRING SONG

Skill Level: Intermediate

Size

Approximately 36" x 40" (91 cm x 102 cm)

Materials

Worsted Weight Yarn

[100% acrylic, 16 ounces, 1020 yards
(449 grams, 932 meters) per skein]

   1 skein green

Note: *Photographed model made with Lion Brand®
Pound of Love® #156 Pastel Green*

36" size 8 (5mm) circular knitting needle (or
size required for gauge)

Gauge

18 sts = 4" (10 cm) in stockinette (knit 1 row,
purl 1 row)

INSTRUCTIONS

CO 190 sts. Do not join; work back and forth in
rows.

Row 1: K1, (P1, K1) twice, knit to last 5 sts,
K1, (P1, K1) twice.

Row 2: Rep Row 1.

Row 3 (right side): K1, (P1, K1) twice; *K2tog,
K5, (YO, K1, YO, K2) twice, sl 1, K1, PSSO, K1,
P1, K1; rep from * to last 5 sts, K1, (P1, K1)
twice.

Row 4: K1, (P1, K1) twice; *P2tog, P13, P2tog,
K1, P1, K1; rep from * across to last 5 sts, K1,
(P1, K1) twice.

Row 5: K1, (P1, K1) twice; *K2tog, (K4, YO,
K1, YO) twice; K1, sl 1, K1, PSSO, K1, P1, K1;
rep from * to last 5 sts, K1, (P1, K1) twice.

Row 6: Rep Row 4.

Row 7: K1, (P1, K1) twice; *K2tog, K3, YO, K1,
YO, K6, YO, K1, YO, sl 1, K1, PSSO, K1, P1, K1;
rep from * to last 5 sts, K1, (P1, K1) twice.

Row 8: Rep Row 4.

Row 9: K1, (P1, K1) twice; *K2tog, (K2, YO,
K1, YO) twice, K5, sl 1, K1, PSSO, K1, P1, K1;
rep from * to last 5 sts, K1, (P1, K1) twice.

Row 10: Rep Row 4.

Row 11: K1; (P1, K1) twice; *K2tog, K1, (YO,
K1, YO, K4) twice, sl 1, K1, PSSO, K1, P1, K1;
rep from * to last 5 sts, K1, (P1, K1) twice.

Row 12: Rep Row 4.

Row 13: K1, (P1, K1) twice; *K2tog, YO, K1,
YO, K6, YO, K1, YO, K3, sl 1, K1, PSSO, K1, P1,
K1; rep from * to last 5 sts, K1, (P1, K1) twice.

Row 14: Rep Row 4.

Repeat Rows 1 through 14 until afghan
measures approximately 40" (102 cm), ending
by working Row 4.

BORDER

Row 1: K1 (P1, K1) twice, purl to last 5 sts, K1
(P1, K1) twice.

Row 2: K1 (P1, K1) twice, purl to last 5 sts,
(P1, K1) twice.

BO; weave in all yarn ends.

GENERAL DIRECTIONS

Abbreviations and Symbols

Knit patterns are written in a special shorthand, which is used so that instructions don't take up too much space. They sometimes seem confusing, but once you learn them, you'll have no trouble following them.

These are Standard Abbreviations

BB	bobble
Beg	beginning
BO	bind off
CO	cast on
Cont	continue
Inc	increase(ing)
K	knit
K2tog	knit two stitches together
Lp(s)	loop(s)
Lpst	loop stitch
Mm	millimeter(s)
Oz	ounces
P	purl
P2tog	purl two stitches together
Patt	pattern
Prev	previous
PSSO	pass the slipped stitch over
Rem	remain(ing)
Rep	repeat(ing)
Rnd	round
Sl	slip
St(s)	stitch(es)
Tbl	through back loop
Tog	together
YB	yarn in back of needle
YF	yarn in front of needle
YO	yarn over the needle
YRN	yarn around needle

These are Standard Symbols

*An asterisk (or double asterisks**) in a pattern row, indicates a portion of instructions to be used more than once. For instance, "rep from * three times" means that after working the instructions once, you must work them again three times for a total of 4 times in all.

† A dagger (or double daggers ††) indicates that those instructions will be repeated again later in the same row or round.

: The number after a colon tells you the number of stitches you will have when you have completed the row or round.

( ) Parentheses enclose instructions which are to be worked the number of times following the parentheses. For instance, "(K1, P2) 3 times" means that you knit one stitch and then purl two stitches, three times.

Parentheses often set off or clarify a group of stitches to be worked into the same space or stitch.

[ ] Brackets and ( ) parentheses are also used to give you additional information. For instance, "(rem sts are left unworked)".

Terms

Finish off—This means to end your piece by pulling the yarn through the last loop remaining on the needle. This will prevent the work from unraveling.

Continue in Pattern as Established—This means to follow the pattern stitch as if has been set up, working any increases or decreases in such a way that the pattern remains the same as it was established.

Work even—This means that the work is continued in the pattern as established without increasing or decreasing.

Gauge

This is probably the most important aspect of knitting!

Gauge simply means the number of stitches per inch that result from a specified yarn worked with needles in a specified size. But since everyone knits differently—some loosely, some tightly, some in-between—the measurements of individual work can vary greatly, even when the knitters use the same pattern and the same size yarn and or needle.

If you don't work to the gauge specified in the pattern, your project will never be the correct size, and you may not have enough yarn to finish your project. Needle sizes given in instructions are merely guides, and should never be used without a gauge swatch.

To make a gauge swatch, knit a swatch that is about 4" square, using the suggested needle and the number of stitches given in the pattern. Measure your swatch. If the number of stitches is fewer than those listed in the pattern, try making another swatch with a smaller needle. If the number of stitches is more than is called for in the pattern, try making another swatch with a larger needle. It is your responsibility to make sure you achieve the gauge specified in the pattern.

Knitting Needles

Knitting needles in the United States are usually marked with numbers. In most of the rest of the world, knitting needles are indicated with metrics. Here is a guide from the Craft Yarn Council:

US Number	Metric
0	2 mm
1	2.25 mm
2	2.75 mm
3	3.25 mm
4	3.5 mm
5	3.75 mm
6	4 mm
7	4.5 mm
8	5 mm
9	5.5 mm
10	6 mm
10 1/2	6.5 mm
11	8 mm
13	9 mm
15	10 mm
17	12.75 mm
19	15 mm
50	25 mm

Knit Terminology

The patterns in this book have been written using the knitting terminology that is used in the United States. Terms which may have different equivalents in other parts of the world are listed below.

United States	International
Gauge	Tension
Skip	Miss
Yarn over (YO)	Yarn forward (yfwd)
Bind off	Cast off

Standard Yarn Weights

To make it easier for yarn manufacturers, publishers, and designers to prepare consumer-friendly products and for consumers to select the right materials for a project, the following standard yarn weight system has been adopted.

Standard Yarn Weight System
Categories of yarn, gauge, ranges, and recommended needle and hook sizes

Yarn Weight Symbol & Category	0 Lace	1 Super Fine	2 Fine	3 Light	4 Medium	5 Bulky	6 Super Bulky
Type of Yarns in Category	Fingering 10 count crochet	Sock Fingering, Baby	Sport, Baby	DK, Light, Worsted	Worsted, Afghan, Aran	Chunky, Craft, Rug	Bulky, Roving
Knit Gauge Range* in Stockinette Stitch to 4 inches	33-40** sts	27-32 sts	23-26 sts	21-24 sts	16-20 sts	12-15 sts	6-11 sts
Recommended Needle in Metric Size Range	1.5-2.25 mm	2.25-3.25mm	3.25-3.75mm	3.75-4.5mm	4.5-5.5mm	5.5-8mm	8mm and larger
Recommended Needle U.S. Size Range	000-1	1 to 3	3 to 5	5 to 7	7 to 9	9 to 11	11 and larger

* GUIDELINES ONLY: The above reflect the most commonly used gauges and needle or hook sizes for specific yarn categories.

** Lace weight yarns are usually knitted or crocheted on larger needles and hooks to create lacy, openwork patterns. Accordingly, a gauge range is difficult to determine. Always follow the gauge stated in your pattern.

Skill Levels

Yarn manufacturers, publishers, needle and hook manufacturers have worked together to set up a series of guidelines and symbols to bring uniformity to patterns. Before beginning a project, check to see if your skill level is equal to the one listed for the project.

Beginner Projects for first-time knitters using basic knit and purl stitches. Minimal shaping.

Easy Projects using basic stitches, repetitive stitch patterns, simple color changes, and simple shaping and finishing.

Intermediate Projects with a variety of stitches, such as basic cables and lace, simple intarsia, double-pointed needles and knitting in the round needle techniques, mid-level shaping and finishing.

Experienced Projects using advanced techniques and stitches, such as short rows, fair isle, more intricate intarsia, cables, lace patterns, and numerous color changes.